WILLOW SMITH
POP'S NEWEST PRINCESS

By Riley Brooks

SCHOLASTIC INC.

New York   Toronto   London   Auckland
Sydney   Mexico City   New Delhi   Hong Kong

ISBN 978-0-545-36887-2

12 11 10 9 8 7 6 5 4 3 2 1   11 12 13 14 15 16/0

Designed by Becky James

Printed in the U.S.A.

First printing, September 2011   40

TABLE OF CONTENTS

INTRODUCTION

Do you ever wonder what it would be like to have your own hit song on the radio? Or to star in a blockbuster movie? How about to hang out with the coolest stars at fashion shows and movie premieres? Pretty amazing, right?

Well, get ready to find out! This book is your ticket to today's newest singing and acting sensation—Willow Smith—from her superstar family to her first audition to her big music break. It's everything you need to know about Willow—plus tons of photos of the young fashionista-in-training. It's almost as good as hanging out with her on set!

CHAPTER 1 • A STAR IS BORN

Even before she had everyone whipping their hair back and forth, Willow was a star in the making. Born in Los Angeles, California, Willow Camille Reign Smith made her world debut on October 31st, 2000, in a family already familiar with fame.

Willow was named after her dad, Will Smith, just like her brother Jaden was named after their mom, Jada Pinkett Smith. Her half-brother, Trey Smith, was also named after their dad; his full name is Willard C. Smith III.

Both Will and Jada are famous movie, television, and music stars, and big brother Jaden is also following in their footsteps with his acting career. So, Willow had a pretty unusual childhood. Since Willow's parents had such exciting travel and work schedules, they home-schooled Willow and her brother Jaden. That way, brother and sister could always be together with their parents and still stay on top of their schoolwork.

It must have been hard for Willow and her brother not to go to a regular school at first. But now they love having tutors and a small classroom. And sometimes, megastars Tom Cruise and Katie Holmes' daughter Suri stops by for a lesson, too!

At home, the Smith family has two dogs and

three cats. And Willow has her very own pet, a snake named Beauty. One day, Willow went to the pet store to get a frog—and came home with a boa constrictor! When Willow came home with the snake, her dad was shocked and her mom was a little scared. But Willow helped her mom get over her fear.

Family time with the Smiths includes everything from eating dinner at home to attending award shows and movie premieres together. It must be really exciting going to events with so many famous celebrities. When Willow went to a recent Nickelodeon Kids Choice Awards, she got to hang out with stars like Jackie Chan, Taylor Lautner, and Chris Rock. Thankfully, Jaden and Trey are often right there with her in case she gets too starstruck. Not bad for a night out with the family!

Willow's parents have always been really supportive of their kids' dreams. They encourage

their children to pursue all of their interests and help them whenever they can. Also, the Smiths keep their children involved with their own work as often as possible. For instance, when Willow was only four years old, she got to be on the cover of her mom's first children's book, *Girls Hold Up This World*. Willow must have been so excited for the photo shoot with her mom. But this was just the very beginning of Willow's stardom.

It was not long before Willow was bitten by the entertainment bug. She couldn't wait to get started! In an interview about her new music career, Willow told the *Huffington Post*, "I wanted to make a difference now [and] . . . I wanted to be big and famous like my mommy and daddy and help people." Her parents didn't know it yet, but Willow was going to make her mark on the world way before her sweet sixteen!

CHAPTER 2 • ALL IN THE FAMILY

With two parents and a brother already in the entertainment business, it's easy to see where Willow's flair for performance comes from. In fact, it's practically a family tradition. Willow told *W* magazine, "I get my flow from my Daddy, my singing from Mommy, and the camera stuff from both."

Willow's dad, Willard Christopher "Will"

Smith, Jr., is a musician and actor who grew up in Philadelphia, Pennsylvania. When Will was just 12 years old, he discovered his passion for rap music. At 16, he began recording music and eventually went on to have two solo albums go multi-platinum. It's no wonder Willow realized she loved singing at such a young age!

When Will was 21 years old, he started his acting career by landing the lead role in a television show called *The Fresh Prince of Bel-Air*. Beyond his TV days, Will is also famous for blockbuster smashes like *Men in Black, Hancock,* and *I Am Legend*. With an all-around entertainer dad, Willow sure has a lot to look up to.

Willow's mom, Jada, also influenced Willow's love of performing. Jada Koren Pinkett Smith was born in Baltimore, Maryland, and had dreams of becoming an actress. In fact, Jada met Willow's dad while auditioning for a part on *The Fresh Prince of Bel-Air*. Jada has acted in movies like

The Nutty Professor and *Madagascar*. Currently, she stars in *HawthoRNe*, a TV show about a nurse. She is also a member of a band called Wicked Wisdom.

Along with her parents, Willow's brother Jaden is no stranger to stardom. When Jaden was 11, he appeared in the Oscar-nominated movie, *The Pursuit of Happyness*, starring his dad. Jaden

also recently starred in *The Karate Kid* with
Jackie Chan. The whole Smith family got to go to
China while Jaden filmed the movie.

When tracing the beginnings of Willow's
interest in acting, Willow's dad told *People*
magazine, "I think a big part was probably
[seeing] Jaden after *The Pursuit of Happyness*.
She saw what Jaden did, she was like 'I want
that.'" Willow knew it was her time to shine!

CHAPTER 3 • LIGHTS, CAMERA, ACTION!

When Willow decided she wanted to be an actress, her mom and dad were really supportive. In fact, her big screen debut was alongside her dad in the movie *I Am Legend*.

Working on her first movie must have been really hard, especially since Willow was just six years old. But even though she was young, Willow was determined to give it her all. For example, when filming one scene, the temperature was below zero outside. But Willow refused to stop working. Willow's dad told *People* magazine, "Willow was out there . . . and she's cold and she's getting a little irritable. And she looks at me and says, 'Daddy, I don't care how low it goes. I'm going to finish.'" Willow wasn't going to let anything get in the way of her dreams!

After officially breaking into the acting world, seven-year-old Willow's next role was as Countee Garby in the movie, *Kit Kittredge*:

An American Girl Mystery. Once Willow got the part, she was super excited since her pal Abigail Breslin was cast as Kit Kittredge. Willow also had her dad with her on set. "My dad gives me tips . . . .He says listen to the director and feel the moment," Willow told *People* magazine. Her dad's tips definitely paid off: Willow won her first award along with her cast—a 2009 Young Artist Award for Best Performance in a Feature Film – Young Ensemble Cast.

After Kit Kittredge, Willow got to try something totally different—lending her voice to an animated movie. Willow's mom had started working on *Madagascar: Escape 2 Africa*, voicing the part of Gloria, the hippo. When the directors called Jada and asked if Willow would want to come on as a younger version of Gloria, Willow was so excited.

Willow had so much fun playing Baby Gloria. It must have been amazing to see her

voice matched up with animation! "Every time
I would mess up, my mom would laugh, and I
would laugh, and she would stop, and I would
stop," Willow told *The Today Show*. The movie
was a laugh-out-loud hit with many audiences—
making over $60 million its opening weekend!

After *Madagascar 2*, Willow got a part on the TV show *True Jackson, VP*. The show follows the adventures of True Jackson, a 15-year old vice president of a fashion company. Willow was cast as a younger version of True Jackson. In Nickelodeon's announcement about the special episode, Willow shared what she loves about *True Jackson*: "I get my style ideas from *True Jackson, VP*. If I had my own fashion company, I would call it 'Willow's Reign.'" (Reign is one of Willow's middle names.)

The actress who plays True Jackson, Keke Palmer, was also excited to see Willow in the part. Keke loved working with Willow. "She's great. She takes direction so well. At the same time, she's able to have fun!" Keke told *Access Hollywood*. No wonder the girls were such good friends on set.

All before the age of ten, Willow had taken on TV and movies. What would the young diva conquer next? Singing, of course!

When Willow had officially made her debut in the acting world, she already had experience as a singer! Willow lent her voice to one of her dad's songs when she was four years old. Willow told the *Daily Record,* "I recorded a song with Daddy and only said a couple of words and I thought, 'This is cool.'" Willow was already on track to have her own music career.

When Willow was five, the Smith family followed the Ozzfest tour to support mom's heavy metal band, Wicked Wisdom. Willow got to watch her mom perform on stage and loved it! Willow knew she wanted to make music when she saw how much fun her mom was having. "I thought, 'Maybe I should do that.' So I did," Willow explained to the *Daily Record.* The moment Willow realized she wanted to be a singer, she declared her love of music to her parents.

When her first song "Whip My Hair" came out, it was a smash hit! It placed #11 on the Billboard Hot 100—the highest position a newcomer had ever taken! Even older bro Jaden likes the song. In an interview with Just Jared he said, "I think it's really really cool. I think a lot of people will be whipping their hair back and forth. I don't know about anybody else, but my neck hurts a little bit!"

Going from just a few words on her dad's song to her very own song "Whip My Hair" was a dream come true for Willow. In an interview with Radio Disney, Willow described what it was like recording her first song, noting "it was a phenomenal experience. Like when I was recording it . . . it took some time but it became so big and so awesome it was really fun." Willow worked very hard on the song and is especially attached to the meaning. "'Whip My Hair' means don't

be afraid to be yourself . . . and don't let anybody tell you that that's wrong. Because the best thing is you," she told MTV.

When Willow released her song, she was also in talks for a record deal with one of the biggest stars in the music business—Jay-Z. Soon after

"Whip My Hair" was released, Jay-Z signed Willow to his record label Roc Nation, which has managed everybody from Rihanna to the Ting Tings to Beyoncé's younger sister, Solange Knowles. In an interview with *Yahoo Music*, Willow talked about what it was like to work with Jay-Z: "When I have an idea, and I express it to him, he doesn't say, 'Oh, that's bad. I don't like it. That's bad.' He tries to make it better." It must be so great for Willow to have such an awesome mentor.

Record her first song? Check. Score a record deal? Check. Next up? Making the video!

CHAPTER 5 • TOPPING THE CHARTS

From releasing "Whip My Hair" to getting signed to Roc Nation, Willow's music career was off to a fast start. Making the music video for her song was the next step—and she had to get the video out quickly! For Willow, making the video was hard work. But the toughest part was the choreography. Willow told interviewers from the TV show *106 and Park* that on the first day at the music video shoot, she kept thinking to her-

self, "I hope I don't mess up, I hope I don't slip and fall and get dizzy!"

Willow practiced the moves over and over again for three weeks and wouldn't stop until she mastered them. Thankfully, her mom and best friends were there for support. "Having my Warriorettes there, my best friends caring—Jade, Angel Punky, they're all just my best friends—and my family there just made it even better," Willow explained to *MTV News*. "Warriorettes" is the nickname Willow uses for her best friends and it has a special meaning. "It takes a warrior to stand up for themselves and not let anybody tell them that what they're wearing or what they're saying or what they're doing is wrong," she explained to *MTV News*.

Aside from having awesome dance moves, Willow wanted to make sure her video was positive and full of energy. She got her wish when Ray Kay, the director of Justin Bieber's "Baby" music video, signed on to direct. When describing the video to Just Jared, Ray explained, "Everyone is in a gray world. Then Willow comes in full of color and personality and energy and changes the world."

Willow debuted her video on *106 and Park* on the BET network. In her interview on the show, Willow talked about some of the thoughts she had while shooting the video. On set, she told herself, "This is my dream. So it doesn't matter if I fall a little bit!" Her courageous attitude paid off and within one day, the YouTube video had over 100,000 views. Today, the number of YouTube views is well over 30 million.

With viewers in the millions, Willow was rocketed to super stardom in only a few days. When asked about what it's like entering the limelight, she told Ryan Seacrest in a radio interview, "It's very, very amazing, and it's very overwhelming!" Willow's song was so popular, her fans began posting their own YouTube versions of "Whip My Hair"! With a growing fan base that includes superstars like Britney Spears, Selena Gomez, and Justin Bieber, Willow is well on her way to taking over the music industry!

CHAPTER 6 • FUNKY FASHIONISTA

As much as Willow loves acting and singing, Willow's style is making her one of the most talked about young celebrities today. From her hair to her clothes and accessories—Willow is always trying something new.

"I used to like dresses and tights but when

I turned nine, my style changed," Willow told *Teen Vogue*. Nowadays, Willow calls her style "schoolgirl meets punk rock" and she's had some pretty cool outfits. She's been known to wear black lace-up pants, one-shouldered corsets, and even leather gloves!

Willow's funky style doesn't just stop at her clothes. She is always trying something new with her hair. One time, Willow secured her parent's permission to get a half-shaven, half-straight bob that totally had fashion magazines buzzing. Even beyond the bob, Willow has tried heart-shaped do's, purple hair, and even red and white candy cane twists for a holiday tree lighting for the LA Kings Holiday Ice in Los Angeles. She is definitely not afraid to try different styles!

Accessories are also a fun way Willow changes up her fashion. At big brother Jaden's *Karate Kid* premiere in Paris, Willow wore safety pin earrings! Heads turned when Willow showed

off her nails that had a 3-D effect in an interview with *Access Hollywood.* She loves to mix and match the different sets of these press-on nails.

One thing in her closet Willow cannot live without is her shoes. Her favorite pair? "They're high-tops and they have checkers on the bottom and they're like yellow and pink and white and they're so tight!" Willow gushed to *MTV News*.

Willow is still a newbie to the fashion world, but she's already sat in the front row at Milan Fashion Week sandwiched between mom Jada and supermodel Naomi Campbell! Willow told *Teen Vogue*, "Milan Fashion Week was fun because I saw how the designers are all so different. Say Dolce and Gabbana, most of their designs were delicate and more fitted, but compared to someone else like Ferragamo, their stuff was different." Willow already speaks like a pro in the fashion world!

Willow turns to English rock star Billy Idol for her style inspiration, and loves the leather, studs, and black he wore. She also likes Rihanna's and Lady Gaga's styles. Willow's idols may have influenced her look, but just like her message in "Whip My Hair," she's the first to point out how important it is to be an individual. Willow is definitely way ahead of the fashion curve!

So what is life like for Willow? As normal as it can be! Even though Willow is often in the spotlight, hanging out with her friends is really important to her. Willow loves to spend time with her Warriorettes and best friends Simrin, Jade, and Angel Punky. They were in her "Whip My Hair" video and are always by her side at performances.

Along with hanging out with friends, Willow loves doing regular kid things like playing videogames, reading, and going on swings—that is if she can fit it into her busy schedule! Willow said on *106 and Park*, "In LA on Mondays, I go to school, come back, piano lessons, singing lessons, rehearsals." She also squeezes in tutoring sessions to stay on top of her schoolwork.

With a full schedule, Willow always finds time to do one of her favorite things: shop!

Bloomingdale's, H&M, Forever 21, and Love Culture are some of her favorite stores, and she loves going to New York City to get her shopping on. Designing clothes is another one of Willow's passions. "I always draw clothes at home. I have a sewing machine and I have made my own pajamas – they're pink with Christmas frogs on. It would be cool to have my own line in the future," Willow explained to *InStyle UK* magazine.

Willow and big bro Jaden are also very active as Youth Ambassadors with Project Zambi, a charity that raises money for the 15 million kids in the world who have lost parents and relatives to AIDS. Willow is very proud to be a part of Project Zambi since it's about kids and for kids. On ProjectZambi.org Willow says, "even from the other side of the world, kids in Africa will know they have friends who care about them."

But Willow's main hobby and focus right now is her music. She loves going to concerts with her family to see other performers, even sneaking onstage for a dance-off with honorary big brother Justin Bieber at his concert. Willow is really close to brother Jaden, and her family is a huge part of her daily life. They keep each other grounded, no matter how much of a superstar each kid becomes!

CHAPTER 8 · WHAT'S WILLOW WHIPPIN' UP NEXT?

After releasing "Whip My Hair," Willow scored a bunch of great performances like *Dick Clark's New Year's Rockin' Eve*. At this televised party, Willow rang in the new year with stars like Drake, Ke$ha, Ne-Yo, and Avril Lavigne. Willow even flew onstage on a huge boom box! She also got to perform at the LA tree lighting ceremony with dad Will rocking out in the crowd.

Beyond performances, Willow's style has landed her photo shoots with the *Sunday Times* in London and *Vanity Fair*. She's still going strong with making appearances at events where everyone's eager to see what new outfit she's whipped up!

Willow joined Justin Bieber on the European leg of his tour. She was so excited to go on tour with him and also has lots of cool ideas for her own concert one day, inspired by none other than Taylor Swift's sets on her tours. "I want the stage to just open and have fire coming out!" she told Radio Disney.

In March, Willow won a NAACP award for Outstanding New Artist. Previous winners include Kanye West and Jennifer Hudson. Everyone's definitely taking notice of her!

Musically, Willow is gearing up for the debut

of her first studio album. While she can't reveal
what the songs will be, she told *Yahoo Music*,
"they're going to have messages in them like
'Whip My Hair.'" Willow has worked on a new
song called "Rockstar" and rumors are swirling
that she may remake her dad's Grammy-winning
hit "Parents Just Don't Understand." Dad's musical partner DJ Jazzy Jeff and British songwriter

Jessie J (who has worked with Miley Cyrus, Justin Timberlake, and Alicia Keys) have also been tapped to work on the album. Willow already has some dream collaborations in mind. "[Somebody] I would really want to work with on a song would be Lady Gaga," said Willow in a radio interview on Power 105.1. "She's just so amazing, she's a free person."

Willow has big dreams about the future. While her acting career is currently on hold, Willow has teamed up with dad Will and mentor Jay-Z to play the lead role in a remake of *Annie*, the classic musical. In the meantime, Willow is going full speed ahead with her music career. Willow told *MTV News*, "I would like to be a very well-known artist. . . .I'd like to be a big rock star." With her stellar personality and electric stage presence, Willow is sure to be on top no matter what she sets out to conquer!

CHAPTER 9 • JUST THE FACTS

Full Name: Willow Camille Reign Smith

Birthday: October 31st, 2000

Hometown: Los Angeles, California

Parents: Will and Jada Smith

Siblings: Jaden and Trey Smith

Pets: Two dogs, three cats and a snake (boa constrictor named Beauty)

Best Friends: brother Jaden, her Warriorettes

Music Inspirations: Mom, Dad, Beyoncé, Rihanna, Lady Gaga, Billy Idol, Jay-Z

Favorite Foods: Microwaved pepperoni with cheese

Favorite "Whip My Hair" Hairstyle: Cotton candy hairstyle

Favorite Shoes: Checkered high-tops

Favorite Fashion Designers: Mariel Haenn and Rob Zangardi

Fashion Idols: Billy Idol, Lady Gaga

Lucky Number: 44

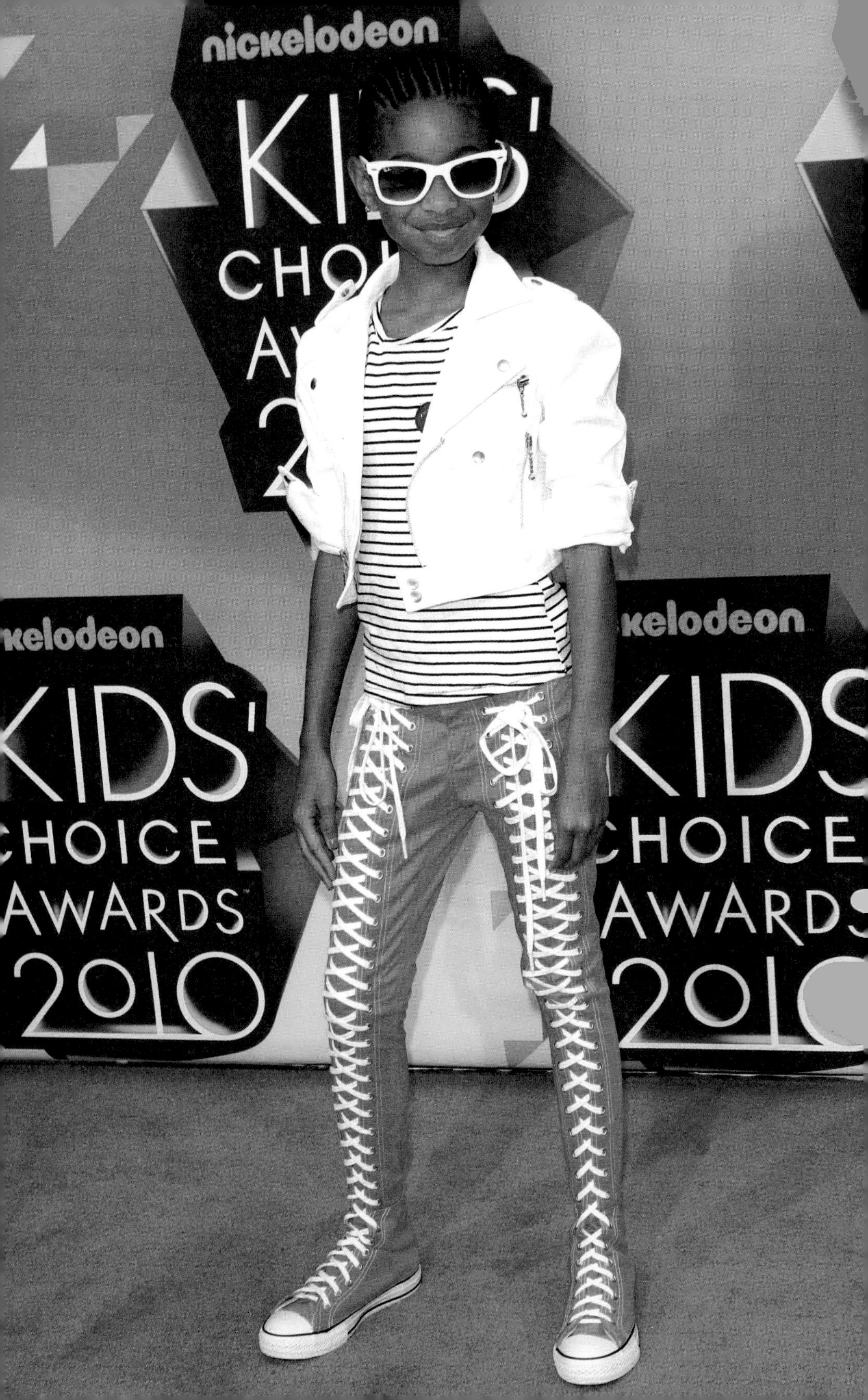
nickelodeon
KIDS'
CHOICE
AWARDS
2010